WHAT'S INSIDE?

PLANES

A DK PUBLISHING BOOK

www.dk.com

Conceived, edited, and designed by DK Direct Limited

Note to parents

What's Inside? Planes is designed to help young children understand the workings of planes, from the turn of the century to the present day. It shows what was inside an early airship, how a jumbo jet can carry hundreds of people speedily around the world, and how flying in an ultralight might feel like hanging from a kite. It is a book for you and your child to read and talk about together, and to enjoy.

Editor Hilary Hockman
Designers Juliette Norsworthy and Helen Spencer
Typographic Designer Nigel Coath
U.S. Editor Laaren Brown
Illustrators Ray Hutchins/Linden Artists, Icon Design Solutions,
Chris Lyon, Jon Sayer, Brian Watson/Linden Artists
Photographers Mike Jerram (cover and page 6), Gary Kevin, Matthew Ward
Written by Alexandra Parsons
Consultants Andrew Nahum and Kelvin Wilson
Design Director Ed Day
Editorial Director Jonathan Reed

First American Edition, 1992. Reprinted 1994

2 4 6 8 10 9 7 5 3 1

Published in the United States by
DK Publishing, Inc.
95 Madison Avenue
New York, New York 10016

Library of Congress Cataloging-in-Publication Data
Planes- 1st American ed.
    p. cm. - (What's Inside?)
Summary: Describes some of the external and internal workings of such crafts as an airship, a helicopter, a jumbo jet, and an ultralight plane.
ISBN: 1-56458-135-7 (hardcover) 0-7894-4296-5 (paper)
1. Airplanes – Juvenile literature. 2. Aeronautics – Juvenile literature.
[1. Aeronautics 2. Airplanes.] I. Series.
TL547.P53 1992
629.133 — dc20   92 - 52831 CIP AC
Printed in Italy

WHAT'S INSIDE?
PLANES

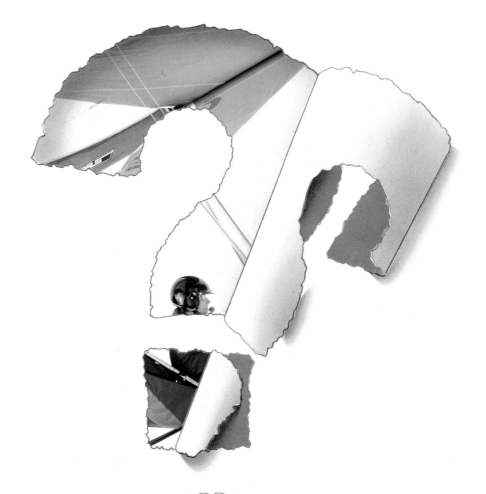

DK

DK PUBLISHING, INC.

AIRSHIP

Airships stay in the air because they are full of a special gas that keeps them up. Today, airships float around like big billboards in the sky, advertising different things. Sixty years ago they carried passengers, but the lighter-than-air gas wasn't as safe as the kind used today.

These movable panels at the back were used to steer the airship, like a rudder steers a boat.

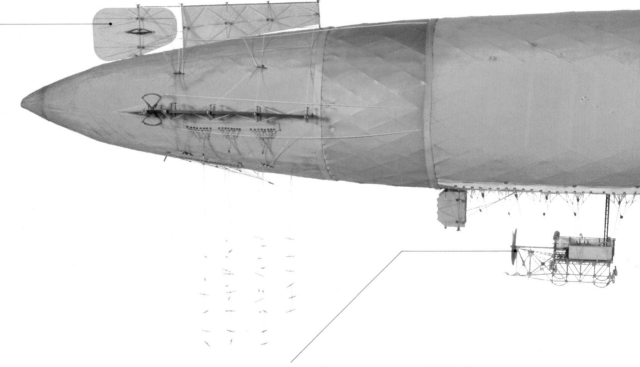

Each car or gondola hanging underneath the airship had an engine. The engines turned the propellers and kept the airship moving forward.

The gas in an airship is lighter than air, just like the gas in toy balloons that float up and away unless you hold on tight.

Airships had to be as lightweight as possible. They were covered in cotton cloth.

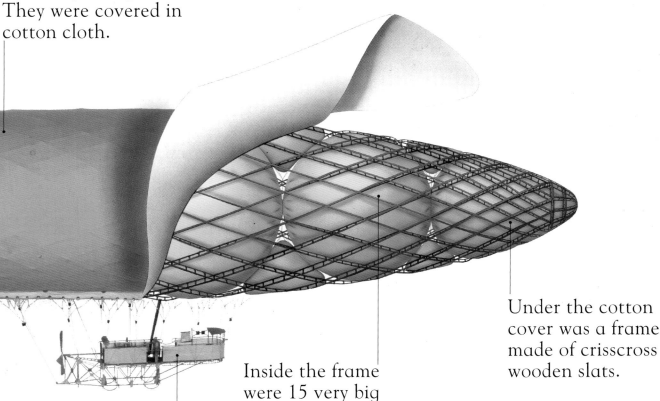

Under the cotton cover was a frame made of crisscross wooden slats.

Inside the frame were 15 very big gas balloons.

Passengers and crew were carried in this gondola.

Flying over land, the pilot used a map to figure out where the airship was traveling. He just leaned over the edge of the gondola looking for roads, rivers, and other landmarks.

EARLY PLANE

The body of this plane is made of wood, fabric, wires, and glue! It's hard to believe it now, but somehow, nearly 100 years ago, a Frenchman named Louis Blériot flew this flimsy little craft 23½ miles across the English Channel.

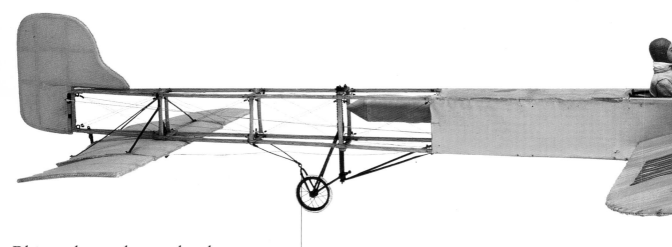

Blériot knew how wheels were attached to bicycles. He copied this idea to attach the wheels to his plane.

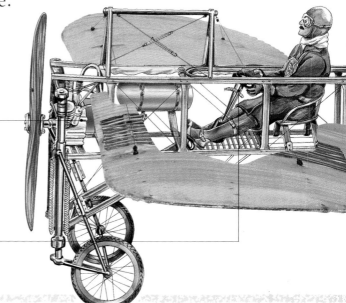

The engine turned a big wooden propeller, and that moved the plane forward.

The pilot controlled the plane from the cockpit. From here he could move the wires that steered the plane.

Once this plane had made a successful flight, everyone wanted one! Blériot set up a factory and made 100 just like it.

The wings kept the plane up in the sky, supported by the wind rushing past.

The material covering the wings was shrunk tight onto the framework and sealed with a special waterproof glue.

The rudder steered the plane. It was moved by wires that ran from the controls in the cockpit to the tail.

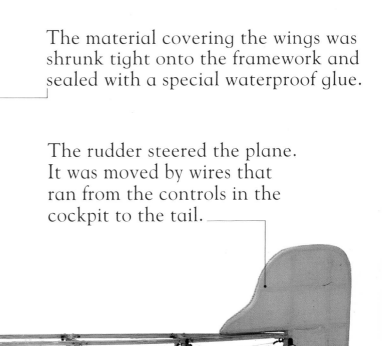

The frame was made of a strong, bendy kind of wood and was held in place by wires.

LIGHT AIRCRAFT

If you've ever been to an air show, you've probably seen a tiny plane like this in the air. This Pitts Special is made for daredevil stunts such as looping the loop. It flies upside down so often that its top and underside are painted different colors so the people on the ground can see which way up it is!

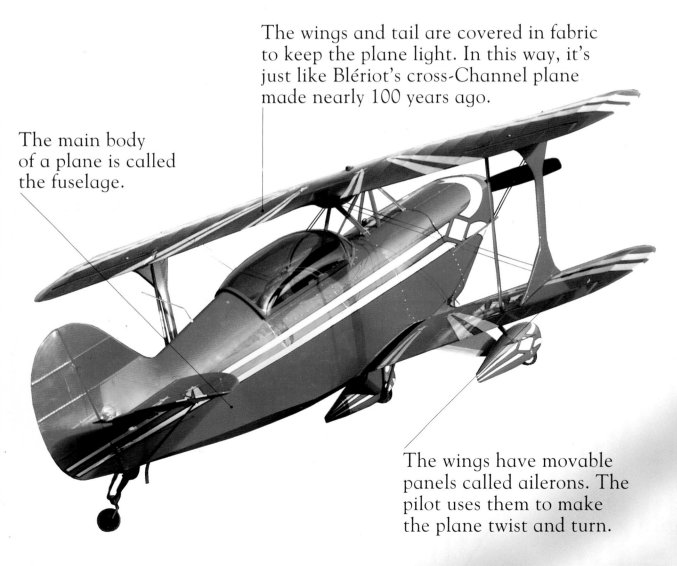

The wings and tail are covered in fabric to keep the plane light. In this way, it's just like Blériot's cross-Channel plane made nearly 100 years ago.

The main body of a plane is called the fuselage.

The wings have movable panels called ailerons. The pilot uses them to make the plane twist and turn.

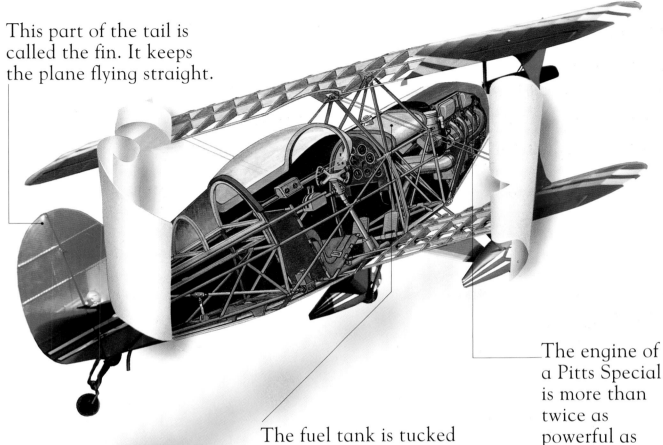

This part of the tail is called the fin. It keeps the plane flying straight.

The engine of a Pitts Special is more than twice as powerful as the engine of a family car.

The fuel tank is tucked away here. Pipes take the fuel to the engine.

Diesel oil and dye in the exhaust pipes make the colored smoke that comes out during an air show.

This is a pretty spectacular trick! It's called wing-walking.

Lots of Pitts Specials are built at home by people using kits.

FLYING BOAT

In the days before modern jets, air travel was luxurious and leisurely. Planes had to stop frequently to take on supplies and fuel. There weren't many airports – they cost a lot of money to build – so planes were built that could land on water.

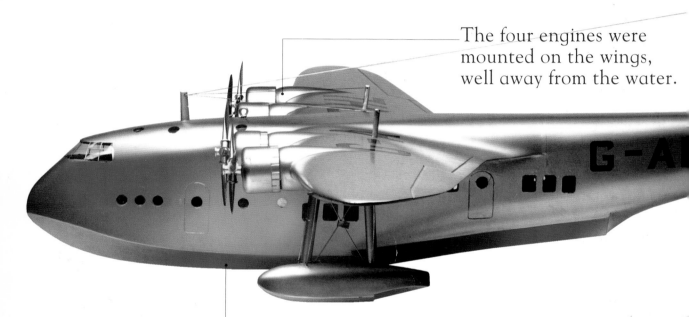

The four engines were mounted on the wings, well away from the water.

The underside of a flying boat is called the hull. Not surprisingly, it was shaped like the bottom of a boat.

The captain and the radio operator sat here, in the cockpit.

On some flights, passengers didn't have to sleep in their seats. The plane would land in the evening and everyone would go to a luxury hotel nearby.

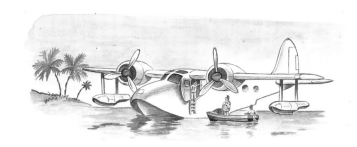

This is the lounge, with tables, comfortable chairs, and vases of fresh flowers.

Freshly cooked meals were prepared in a real kitchen by a chef.

In the mailroom, the postman sorted letters and packages, ready for delivery at the next stop.

HELICOPTER

This helicopter is an air ambulance. Helicopters can land and take off from just about anywhere, so an air ambulance can rescue people from the most awkward places, like the top of a mountain or a life raft bobbing in the sea. An injured person can be rushed to the hospital in minutes.

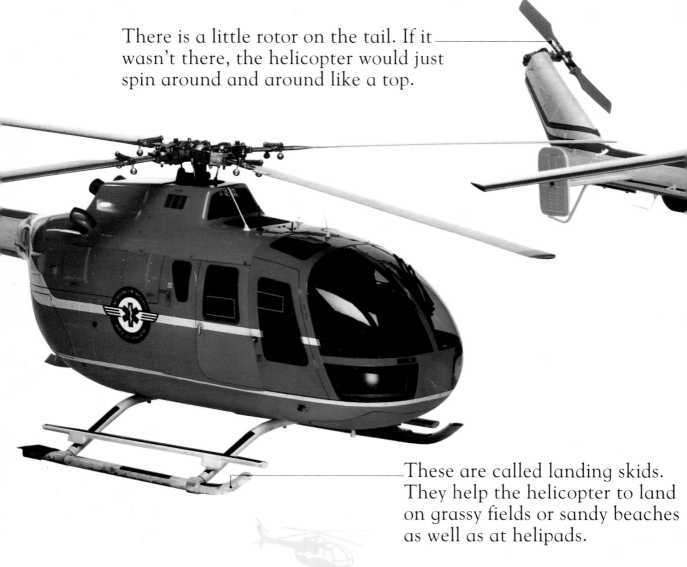

There is a little rotor on the tail. If it wasn't there, the helicopter would just spin around and around like a top.

These are called landing skids. They help the helicopter to land on grassy fields or sandy beaches as well as at helipads.

The letter H painted on top of the lighthouse makes it easier for the helicopter pilot to see where to land.

Helicopters have rotor blades instead of ordinary wings. The blades whiz around so fast that the air rushing past lifts the helicopter into the sky.

The powerful engine uses up fuel very quickly. Helicopters can't stay in the air for long without coming down to refuel.

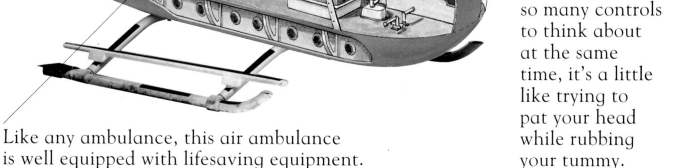

Flying a helicopter is tricky. There are so many controls to think about at the same time, it's a little like trying to pat your head while rubbing your tummy.

Like any ambulance, this air ambulance is well equipped with lifesaving equipment.

JUMBO JET

Modern jets are crisscrossing the world all the time, taking people from place to place quickly and efficiently. This jumbo jet is one of the biggest airplanes ever made. It can carry more than 500 people.

Children have lots to do on planes. The cabin crew gives them games and crayons while the grown-ups watch a movie or listen to music on headphones.

Food is prepared in kitchens on the ground, then heated up in the galleys on board.

There's an upstairs and a downstairs on a jumbo jet.

Passengers' suitcases are put in cargo holds.

Seats are attached to the floor. They tip back so passengers can rest. Babies sometimes travel in special cribs.

All aboard! Tickets please! Modern jets provide transportation almost like your local bus service.

There are no propellers on a jet. The engines move the plane forward by sucking in air at the front and pushing it out the back.

Jets fly high above the clouds where the air is very cold and where you can't breathe. The plane is completely sealed so the windows don't open.

FIGHTER PLANE

Fighter planes like this F16 have to move quickly and quietly so they can sneak up on the enemy and get out of the way fast if danger strikes. Some modern jet fighters can even fly backward. They can climb high or dive low, skimming the tops of trees.

A fighter plane can have its fuel topped off while it's flying along.

The pilot sits in an ejector seat. If the plane is about to crash, the pilot pulls a lever and...whoosh! The canopy flies off, the seat shoots out, and a parachute opens.

The pilot sits tilted back to avoid passing out if the fighter turns very suddenly.

The nose cone contains the instruments for guiding weapons and for tracking other planes.

Air rushes into the jet engine here. It comes out through the jet pipe.

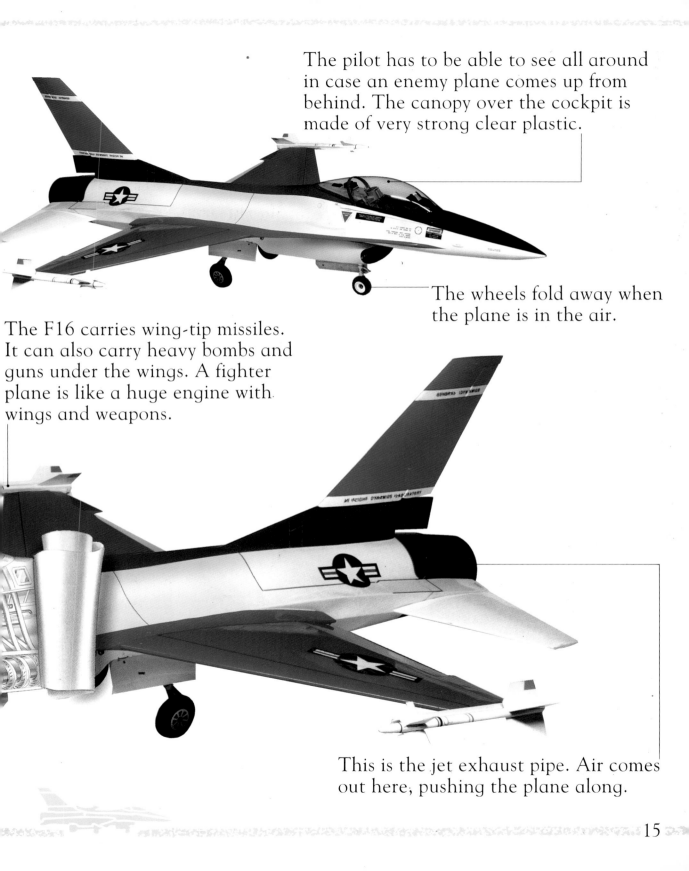

The pilot has to be able to see all around in case an enemy plane comes up from behind. The canopy over the cockpit is made of very strong clear plastic.

The wheels fold away when the plane is in the air.

The F16 carries wing-tip missiles. It can also carry heavy bombs and guns under the wings. A fighter plane is like a huge engine with wings and weapons.

This is the jet exhaust pipe. Air comes out here, pushing the plane along.

ULTRALIGHT

An ultralight is like a huge kite powered by a little engine. You can travel at about 50 miles an hour and up to 20,000 feet high in one of these. Many people fly them for fun, but in Africa they are being used to spot illegal hunters of elephants and rhinos.

The wing is made of material held in shape by aluminum tubes called ribs.

The cockpit is made of fiberglass, a strong but light plastic.

The engine makes the propeller spin.

This is the engine. The very first ultralight was made from a hang glider and a chainsaw motor!

Haven't you ever wished you could climb on a kite and fly above the treetops? That's what flying in an ultralight feels like.

The pilot pulls the control bar back to fly faster and pushes it forward to slow down.

The instruments tell the pilot how fast and how high the ultralight is flying.

Seat belts hold the pilot and passenger safely in their seats.

The passenger sits here, behind the pilot. They both wear crash helmets and warm clothing.

This throttle pedal controls the amount of fuel that gets to the engine. The pilot uses it to rev the engine for takeoff and to climb high in the air.